I Am Simon

The Untold Story of Simon of Cyrene

By Anne-Marie Klobe

Pictures by Mauro Lirussi

Nihil Obstat
John Froula, Ph.D.,
Censor librurum deputatis

Imprimatur
Bernard A. Hebda
Archbishop of Saint Paul and Minneapolis
August 6, 2021

Illustrations by Mauro Lirussi

ISBN 978-1-7378808-0-6 (Print/Hardback)
ISBN 978-1-7378808-1-3 (Print/Paperback)
ISBN 978-1-7378808-2-0 (eBook)

I Am Simon
The Untold Story of Simon of Cyrene

By Anne-Marie Klobe
Pictures by Mauro Lirussi

This book is dedicated to my dad, Jim Klobe,
who patiently carried his cross until he took
his last breath,
and to all other people who lost their lives in
2020 and 2021.

Eternal rest grant unto them, O Lord,
and let perpetual light shine upon them.
May the souls of all the faithful departed,
through the mercy of God, rest in peace.
Amen.

Then Jesus said to his disciples, *"If any of
you want to come with me, you must forget
yourself, carry your cross, and follow me."*

—Matthew 16:24

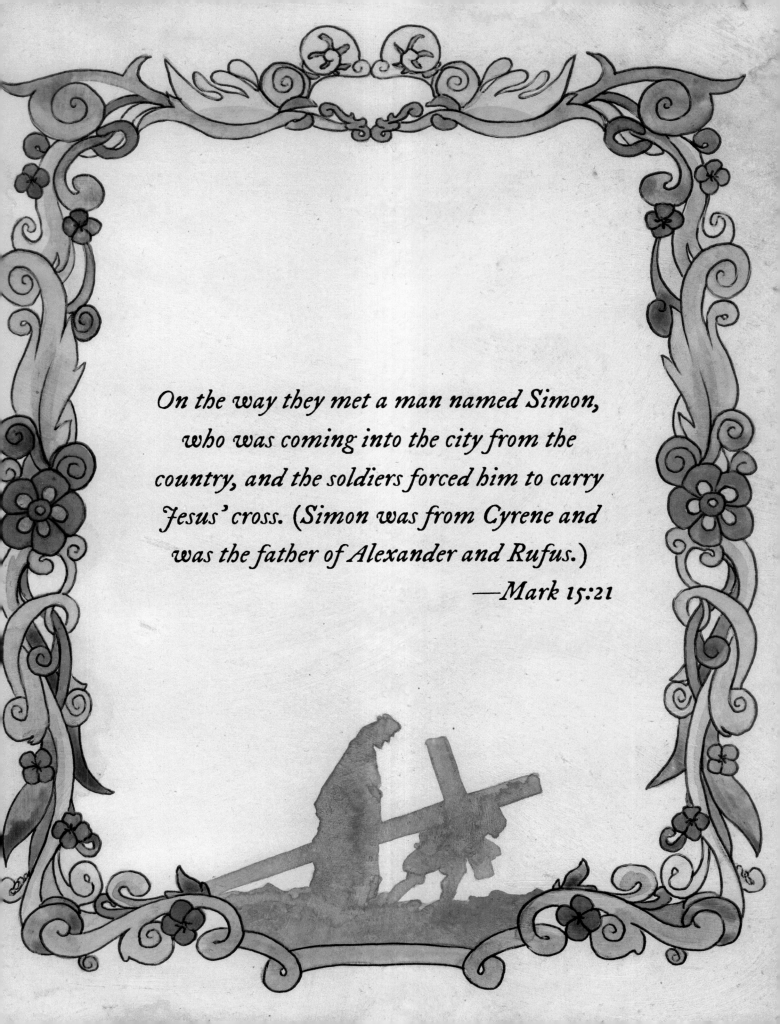

On the way they met a man named Simon, who was coming into the city from the country, and the soldiers forced him to carry Jesus' cross. (Simon was from Cyrene and was the father of Alexander and Rufus.)

—Mark 15:21

I, Simon of Cyrene, left my home early Friday morning, before sunrise, after doing some work around the farm. I had milked the goats, gathered some eggs, and pulled out a few weeds before packing up my old faithful donkey and setting off for Jerusalem.

My two sons, Alex and Rufus, lived in the city, so I was heading out to spend the weekend with them for the Sabbath, planning to come back on Monday to resume my duties. My heart was heavy, since this would be my first year without my beloved wife, Miriam, who had died ten months before. Nevertheless, I persevered.

The trek was arduous because the road was scattered with sharp rocks, snakes were slithering around everywhere, and one never knew who you might meet along the way. But I had traveled this route multiple times, ever since my sons moved to the city for work.

Before long, I saw the glittering gold of the Jerusalem temple.

I was so close, maybe only half a mile from where I planned to meet Alex and Rufus, just on the other side of town in a small Mediterranean inn.

Suddenly, I came to a stop. Something was very different. There was a strange stillness in the air, interrupted by the hum of a crowd of some sort down the hill from where my donkey and I were standing.

As I walked closer, I heard jeers, taunting, and yells. I wanted to stay focused on my mission, but my curiosity got the better of me.

What's going on? I wondered.

After tying my donkey to an empty post, I quietly rounded the corner of an old bakery, where a thick mob was blocking my sight.

Is this some type of parade?

Yet, it didn't seem joyful and light, the way a parade usually feels, and the Sabbath was in just a couple of days.

When I took a few steps forward, I heard a woman gasp: "Look! He's talking to his mother."

Another woman said, "No, that can't be his mom, she's too young."

As I peered through the crowd, I saw the bloody back of a man carrying a large cross, with a woman standing in front of him. She was overcome with grief, as I could tell from the teary streaks on her face. Strangely, she looked as if she were also encouraging him.

I was just opposite her, and tried to get closer, when I heard a loud thud on the ground. Then I was forcefully pushed forward.

"This man will help," a gruff voice behind me said as I stumbled out into the street, nearly tripping over rocks and pebbles. As I caught startled glances from the people around me, I saw the man lying face down on the ground, crushed under the cross. His head was covered with a helmet of thorns.

Then a memory came to mind. A few years back, I was outside watering my fig trees on a hot day in June. Miriam had come home from a walk in the countryside. Her eyes glistened as she told me that she had come across a large group of people listening intently to a man telling a story on a grassy hill.

The storyteller told of a Samaritan who happened to come across a half-beaten traveler. While others passed by, the Samaritan stopped and helped the wounded traveler, pouring wine and oil over his cuts, and bandaging them. Then, the Samaritan brought the wounded man back to an inn, where he recovered. I remembered smiling when I heard the story, and resolved to do something similar someday.

But today was not going to be that day. I didn't have time to help anyone. I just wanted to see my sons, and I was running late.

Just then, the man lifted his head off the ground and looked up at me through eyelids that were almost swollen shut. I felt as if he had known me from the moment I was born. His face expressed severe agony as blood dripped from his forehead, where the thorns were pushing into his skin. Blood had soaked through every inch of his clothing, and his legs had been scourged with nails.

I lifted his cross, which looked like it was made of olive wood—very rough, as if it had been cut down in a hurry. As splinters dug into my hands, I winced in pain. Then I noticed his right shoulder, where the skin had been rubbed away. I could even see the whites of his bones. The man didn't speak a single word, but I was certain that he shouldn't have been sentenced as he had been.

As I walked along with him, step by step, I was so focused on the treacherous road that I wasn't aware of a woman right in front of me until I brushed into her faded blue robe. Her arms were outstretched as she pressed her veil against the man's face, which by now had become a pool of blood and sweat. When she briefly removed her veil, I saw a replica of his face emblazoned on the cloth.

Who is he? This man must be well known, for many people seem to love him—although many others do not.

When women came up to him, crying tears of sadness, he spoke to them softly.

"Do not weep for me," he said, "but weep for yourselves and for your children."

We continued walking—or rather, struggling—around the sharp corners of the street. Often, one or two men would jump into his path, calling him horrible names and spitting on him.

I began to think of my own troubles in life. My eyes filled with tears as I thought of the future of Jerusalem. I worried about my friends who were sick, those who were lonely, some who were dying from leprosy, and I was especially concerned for my sons. *What will they do without me?* And as the cross almost fell upon my own back, I began to be convinced that no matter the reputation, accusation, or circumstance of a person, nobody should ever have to carry his cross alone.

The man appeared to be very focused, almost in prayer, and although the cross was heavy, the sorrow and worry that was burdening my heart seemed to lift with each step that I took. It was like I was united with this man, and somehow his suffering seemed to pour mercy out on the whole world—not just over my own heart. I was so distracted by my thoughts that I didn't see a stone in front of me, so I tripped and fell. He tripped, too, crying out in pain as he cut open his knee. A group of onlookers laughed at us both. I felt humiliated, and I can't imagine how he felt.

Finally, we reached the top of a hill outside the gate.

"Make way for the king!" mocked one of the soldiers, dressed in red and wearing golden armor.

"What took so long?" jeered another.

I noticed a young man supporting a woman whom I recognized from earlier as his mother. She had a strength and a feminine grace about her, even while her son was being violently stripped of all his clothes, which reopened every wound as they tore off the scabs.

Unable to bear this scene any longer, I ran back through the gate to the city. Along the way, I passed hundreds of people, some with their eyes glazed over, others with tear-filled eyes, and still others who looked completely shocked.

By the time I arrived at the inn, I was a few hours late. Alex and Rufus weren't there, so I figured they must be out somewhere looking for me. When I ran through the labyrinthian streets, calling their names, the sky suddenly went dark as the sun literally stopped shining.

What is going on?

I nearly lost my balance as I blindly pressed into the stone walls of storefronts to guide me.

"Dad, where are you?"

Rufus's frightened voice was yelling as he heard me crying out for him and his brother. When we found each other in the dark, the three of us embraced, then stumbled through the blackness until we found Alex's house.

After managing to pull together a simple meal of bread, olives, and cheese, I hardly touched my food, although I was hungry from the journey. Instead of eating, I told my boys about what I had seen in the street.

"Oh, I've heard of that man," Rufus said.

"Yes," Alex chimed in. "He claims to be the Son of God. But don't worry, Dad. We don't believe him. We're still waiting for the God of Moses to come."

I was beginning to have my doubts, but at that point, I was just glad to be with my family, although I really missed Miriam.

Shortly after lunch, as we were resting, a thunderous noise echoed throughout Jerusalem. The table and chairs started shaking, and a canvas painting of my beloved family crashed to the floor. I lit a torch and ran to the door to observe the scene in front of me. People were frantically running through the streets, pounding their chests. I recognized the voice of a high priest, screaming, "The curtain in the temple has just been torn in half!"

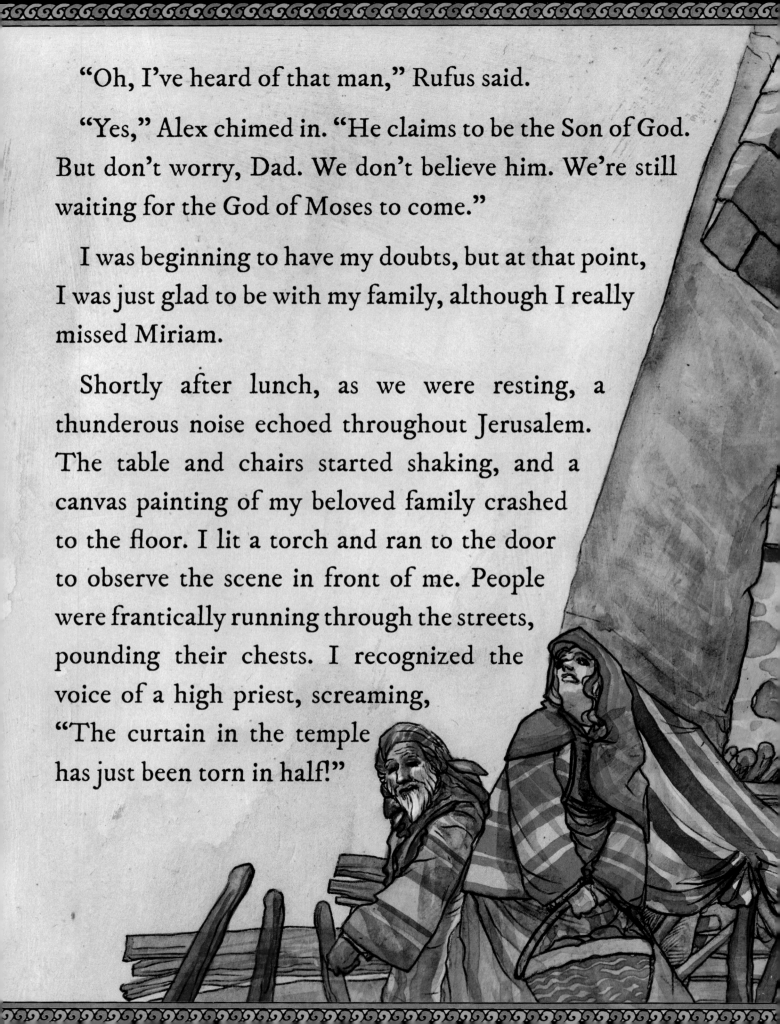

I was shocked, for I had seen that curtain years before. It was six inches thick, nearly six stories high, and required three hundred priests to lift it up and move it into place.

And now, it's torn?!? Just this morning, I was milking goats, and now the sky is pitch black, and I'm in the middle of an earthquake! What more can happen?

When I went back inside, I saw terror reflected on my sons' faces. As we huddled together, we closed our eyes and prayed that the end of the world would not come quite yet.

I have things to do! I want to see my sons get married, and I can hardly wait to become a grandfather!

Suddenly, I felt a strange presence in the room and heard a voice whisper to me, "Simon..., Simon.... What you did today was very good. For your charity, you will be talked about for thousands of years."

I opened my eyes, and standing before me was Miriam! She was glowing with a radiant smile on her face. Then she quickly disappeared.

Surely, that Man WAS the Son of God!

Discussion Questions

1. Have there been times in *your* life when you intended to do something good, but other things got in the way?

2. Miriam listened to a man talk about the Good Samaritan. Who was that man?

3. The Gospel of Matthew mentions the dead appearing to others on Good Friday. How did Miriam's appearance affect Simon?

4. What are some struggles in your life that you can unite with Jesus' suffering?

5. How have you experienced God in others?

6. Can you think of people who need help carrying their cross? How can you help them?

7. There were several Stations of the Cross mentioned in this story. What were they?

Prayer to the Shoulder Wound of Christ

by Thomas D. Beven, Bishop of Springfield, Massachusetts

O Loving Jesus, meek Lamb of God, I, a miserable sinner, salute and worship the most Sacred Wound of Thy Shoulder on which thou didst bear Thy heavy Cross, which so tore Thy flesh and laid bare Thy Bones as to inflict on Thee an anguish greater than any other wound of Thy Most Blessed Body. I adore Thee, O Jesus, most sorrowful, I praise and glorify Thee, and give Thee thanks for this most sacred and painful Wound, beseeching Thee by that exceeding pain, and by the crushing burden of Thy heavy Cross to be merciful to me, a sinner, and to forgive me all my mortal and venial sins, and to lead me on towards Heaven along the Way of The Cross.

Amen.

Your Cross
-St. Francis de Sales

The everlasting God has in His wisdom foreseen from eternity the cross that He now presents to you as a gift from His inmost heart. This cross He now sends you He has considered with His all-knowing eyes, understood with His divine mind, tested with His wise justice, warmed with loving arms and weighed with His own hands to see that it be not one inch too large and not one ounce too heavy for you.

He has blessed it with His holy Name, anointed it with His consolation, taken one last glance at you and your courage, and then sent it to you from heaven, a special greeting from God to you, an alms of the all-merciful love of God.